PARANORMAL PROFILING

MARTHA HAZZARD DECKER

America Star Books

First printing

America Star Books has allowed this work to remain exactly as the author intended, verbatim, without editorial input.

Softcover 9781611025903
PUBLISHED BY AMERICA STAR BOOKS, LLLP
www.americastarbooks.com

Printed in the United States of America

This book is dedicated to my husband, Ken Decker, who always believed I could write and supported me all the way through to the final publication. It's dedicated to my many "book coaches" as I called them; authors TL Jones, Robbie Thomas, and Dr. Rita Louise along with many others who never stopped believing such as friends Tamra Brickey, Nancy Davis, Wendi Cox and Maria Santos. Interesting is that all of them, except Thomas, are part of East Texas Paranormal. They took the time to ask how the book is coming along and remind me to get to work. The many wonderful friends I have and are just too many to list, I believe I'm rich and fortunate because they care enough to keep me going and see it thorough to the end. This book is for y'all…

WHERE TO BEGIN AND WHY I WROTE THIS BOOK

I spent the past 30 years as an investigator of one sort or another and one evening my brain lit up when that comic style light bulb was turned on, by who is my guess as much as anyone else. I began investigating in the mid-eighties as a photojournalist. Even though I had worked with many different people years before that, I didn't really start getting nosy until I switched from network marketing to media. There was a brief period of time before the photojournalism where cable TV came to Dallas and I learned about Public Access TV. Woohoo, I thought, I can make TV shows. I learned what I needed to learn so that I could produce, direct and edit whatever sort of TV program I could dream up. That was a dream even if it was just for public access, which was a lot different in the eighties. I helped as many other public access producers as I could to learn how to work the cameras. After a few shows I felt I had everything down so I could embark on my path of TV shows. This is when I really began to learn how to interview people.

There were three shows that stand out in my mind as being works from my heart and a lot of fun. One was called, *Why are we killing our children?* It was a talk show where I was the host, producer and editor. The show was about car seats and the safety of children before there were laws requiring car seats. I shot on location at a children's store where we went over different types of car seats. I had to interview doctors and even a legislator before and during the show. That's probably where I really began to learn how to dig and ask questions. Then I began to produce, direct and edit a monthly chamber of commerce magazine, long before this type of show was popular. It was done well enough that the paid cable channel took over the show so they could get paid advertising. Boy, did I get aggravated when that happened. However, they did offer me to be a part of the show, without pay, and I turned it down. I was young and that was the wrong decision, but it was mine. Then the favorite show of all was called, *Ray Wylie Hubbard Live at Dallas Palace.* It involved about eight hours of work to record the show. There were three cameras, a crew of 12 and the use of what was then called the Qube van. That was the cable remote van. It seems that I was the first person in the Dallas metroplex to "check out" the van. It was rather hair raising since I was solely responsible for all the equipment. The owner of Dallas Palace received thousands of dollars of free advertising because the club name was on the back wall of the stage. I had a blast putting together the concert with Ray Wylie Hubbard. We went way back to the seventies when I used to play chess with him at the bar of a club in Dallas called Fannie Ann's in between sets. The show was excellent and I would love to have a copy of it. We filmed the show just as VCR's were becoming popular and they were expensive so there wasn't one at my house. Warner Amex owned the cable station when it was show.

From there I decided I wanted to shoot photographs for the local newspapers and had pictures in the Dallas Morning News, Dallas Times Herald and many others as a freelance photographer. I eventually became a staff photographer for a few papers and eventually was assistant editor of one as I made the transition from photography to writing. All the time I was working with print media I learned how to talk with and interview anyone. During that time I managed to photograph three presidents and cover everything from spots to politics.

My circumstances changed around 1985 and along with print media I made a move into volunteering as a reserve police officer. That meant I had the same powers of arrest as paid police. Here came the switch to learning how to interview from a law enforcement angle. I did this for a while and decided to go back into print media again at two of the local papers. Once again I began to hone my experience interviewing all sorts of people. When in 1995 I was awarded an Associated Press first place award for specialty reporting. This was for an article I investigated for a year before putting it into words and it getting published in the paper.

While I was doing that I was also working as a police officer for the department I would eventually retire from in 2007. I stopped writing for the paper in 1999 after my patrol car was hit by an intoxicated driver, causing me to be off work for nine months. Now I have a steel rod in a femur and one screw left to remind me of the crash. When I returned to work I focused on police work and was the detective or investigator until about 2005 when our department got another sergeant who also started to investigate crimes committed in our city. I was sergeant from 1994 until 2000 where I was made assistant chief of police. I was a negotiator and instructor along with many other hats I had to wear before retiring in 2007. I did some undercover work, presented a variety of things from the police department to the city council during monthly meeting and was the public information officer. All of this and the many hundreds or hours of specialized training continued to hone my knowledge of interviewing suspects, victims and witnesses.

When I retired in 2007 I didn't stop working and was once again another investigator. This time it's on the civil side for a State agency. Nearly seven years later, I'm still interviewing victims, alleged perpetrator and witnesses.

In 1999, when I was recovering from the crash, I began conducting paranormal investigations. My ever present friend, Tamra Brickey, was usually at my side. She had to be since she was my driver. The first place we went was Myrtles Plantation in St. Francisville, LA. It seemed that would be a good place to start. It blossomed from there into East Texas Paranormal (ETP) in 2007. When ETP was formed little did I know how many people I would get to know or how many investigations and interviews we would conduct as a team. There was a time when our team was made up of former and current law enforcement. I think this caused us to interview and investigate in a manner different than others. Our mind set was that of someone in law enforcement so we would look deeper than taking someone 100 percent at their word. In other words, we would go into an investigation not looking to prove the client's statements were true, but with an open mind to try and find the cause or problem and help get it sorted out before we closed the case.

One thing led to another until I started attending paranormal conferences and got on Facebook. Our team put together a website, etxhaunted.com, and finally settled on the name we still have today. When I founded the team one of my goals was to develop a good network of trusted individuals who were willing to help us should we need help. This included everything from demonologist to psychic. In doing this I developed a lot of great relationships and made many friends I can call who I trust.

As our network began to grow and I attended more and more conferences I started getting asked to go on radio shows and speak at conferences. My presentation was about interview skills and how to use some of the skill sets used by detectives and switch it into the paranormal field. Most of the radio shows I'm on end up being about the same thing. This is how *Paranormal Profiling* came to life.

My hope is that most readers will be able to come away from this book with at least one idea they haven't thought of when it comes to interviewing clients and witnesses. The knowledge to obtain even more information through reading and attending conferences might grow within the reader. This is a great way to learn and one I have used all of my life. It's important to remember paranormal shows on TV are for entertainment, not always as they seem, often scripted and usually not the best way to learn how to interview and investigate. Enjoy watching TV for what it is, entertainment and happy reading…

Martha Hazzard Decker

CHAPTER 1

SO YOU WANT TO INTERVIEW AND INVESTIGATE

Do you have any medical issues? Do you have any mental problems? Do you drink or do drugs? Sounds like booking questions at the local jail or doctor's office, right? No, these are some of the questions asked by some paranormal investigators while conducting interviews of potential clients. Some of those investigators were a part of law enforcement and detectives at one time or another. Some may still be in the law enforcement field. This is something that has been discussed within the paranormal community.

Some investigators without any law enforcement background may think these are rude questions to ask a client. While other researchers and investigators have a background in criminal investigations and believe these are normal and important questions to ask, along with a number of other questions such as, what was the weather like or what time does it happen. The eyes of the law enforcement paranormal investigator and the mind work differently than most and can be a handy asset to have on a team.

While some investigators may take the client at their word and go into the investigation to find the proof to support the client's claims, former law enforcement paranormal investigators go into the investigation with a different view. They may not be complete skeptics, but they will take what the client claims and look for concrete causes for the claims. As former police officer TL Jones has said, "Until I see it with my own eyes," she is not going to believe it really happened. It's not that she is saying the client isn't truthful; it's that they may believe something to be other than what it really is in reality. Jones wants to be there when the EVP is captured to know without a doubt that the recorder wasn't manipulated. Other researchers say the same thing. Jones now writes paranormal mystery novels and has been on several radio shows discussing not just her books but the police angle to investigations.

There are several books written that can be applied to paranormal investigations which were written for law enforcement. Katherine Ramsland Ph.D. has been to at least one paranormal conference to discuss paranormal investigations and how to conduct them much like you would at a crime scene. In fact, she took the same presentation used to train police and converted it to be applied in the paranormal realm. She is a forensic psychologist and author. One of her books is 'Ghost: Investigating the Other Side'. She has the same philosophy about investigating a scene. Leave no stone unturned and check everywhere for information.

Ramsland mentions in an interview on a website that she has encountered frauds while they were trying to give her a paranormal experience. She is not the only one to encounter frauds and some of the frauds can be the clients. One researcher conducted an investigation where a client wanted the group to find activity at their location. The researcher did something that would be good for all groups to do before an investigation. They researched the property to check on the history of the location. What was discovered was that the old looking house was a new house built to look old and the property never had a building on it prior to the current building. Nothing had been recorded that had ever happened on the property. Investigators went to the location to conduct their investigation with an open mind being aware that there was nothing associated with the building. What they found during the investigation was that the owners had rigged some special effects to make it seem as if the place was indeed full of paranormal activity. The owners wanted the place to be "declared" as haunted so they could market it as a haunted place, hoping to profit with all the notoriety of having a haunted venue. This then brings into question another thought voiced by other investigators, "What makes a place truly haunted?" Researching this may help others decide on what to pay for or not pay for when it comes to visiting commercial haunted locations.

One group that incorporates common police investigative tactics with the paranormal is Missouri Ghost Hunters Society. Brian Lile has 20 years of law enforcement in his background. They use common forensic techniques such as evidence collection, investigative photography and interviewing, according to their webpage. All of this can be used by any paranormal investigator. You can even put together a forensic kit for the paranormal investigation. This helps in debunking and verifying claims. This would include items such as measuring tape or rulers, temperature or thermometer, fingerprint dust, luminal for detecting blood or lack of, camera, recorder and so on. There are a number of online stores that sell forensic equipment.

Processes used by police detectives can help paranormal investigators to understand what is real, mistaken and subjective. An example could be the one of a social worker and a detective visiting the same house at the same time.

During the visit numerous people come and go after a brief visit. The social worker may sit there and think this family seems to have quite the support group while the detective sits there and thinks, "Dope house." There was an interesting article about 'Paranormal Activity and the FBI: how to avoid common investigative pitfalls' recently published. Officers often operate on "gut" feelings during their career. This may even help keep them safe. Their senses are tuned into what's happening around them more than the average person. This can be learned as can crime scene investigations. Many local colleges have police academies or criminal justice classes. This means there will be basic crime scene textbooks that can be purchased. A lot can be learned from those. Then there are online sites where a lot of online investigative information can be gleaned without purchasing anything.

The main focus of this book is to be open minded when going into an investigation without a predisposition that it is or isn't as the client claims. By keeping an open mind and unbiased opinion investigators will be more open to any evidence that does present instead of immediately dismissing something that may become important at a later date. Be sure to get a full interview from the family that includes medical history, interview neighbors without telling them what's going on next door, obtain the names of collaterals who may be witnesses or have been told about incidents and interview them. Work toward corroborating the client's statements. Ask about criminal history, research the history if the building and property. Check old newspaper articles. The library and local paper can be a great source of information. Check with the county to see who has owned the property if the current owner doesn't have that information available. Try to contact former owners and interview them. The list can go on and on but the information obtained can lead to a really great investigations.

CHAPTER 2

BASIC INTERVIEW SKILLS

How to interpret and use nonverbal skills with the client
The hope is that by the time you finish this book you'll be able to have this skill and know what to look for when interviewing. You'll be able to find their "tell" and be able to understand what they aren't saying. Sometimes it can be like a poker game and as you talk pay attention to the client or witness.

How they say what they say, their demeanor or looks can be a big tell as to how serious and truthful they are or if there is more to the story. Some clients have a lot more to tell but are afraid to tell a stranger what may be personal information. If you don't get the whole story it may be rather difficult to conduct a thorough investigation.

If they are nervous you can tell this by watching how they act. Are they looking around a lot? Is their leg moving up and down rapidly? Do you have to pull them back to the conversation because they're all over the place while trying to talk? Do you get good eye contact with them or are they looking away or down? Are they sweating but it's cold? Do they appear nervous or afraid? Some of this can be explained away because they're embarrassed, have mental problems and are afraid to say or maybe have done something they don't want to tell you about. Maybe they merely want attention or hope to get enough notoriety to get on TV. This is what you have to learn to interpret when interviewing people.

Behavior that encourages the client to keep talking

You should be able to understand how your behavior and attitude affects that of the client or witness. It's important to be able to learn how to build rapport with them so you can get the whole story and not bits and pieces.

If you tell the client you'll be there at 5:00 and show up an hour late without calling they may think you don't really care about their problem. When you're late or can't make the appointment be sure to call ahead to reschedule. Some clients have gone out of their way to prepare for the time you'll spend with them. They clean house, arrange for child care or take off from work. Another example would be to keep your phone on vibrate and pay attention to the client and not what's happing on social media or coming across your phone as text messages. By paying more attention to your phone instead of the client you may come across to them as if they're a bother and you don't really want to be there.

When the interviewer gives the client or witness full attention it conveys to them that you care and is serious about helping them with what they see as a problem. It might not be a problem and you may be able to explain how things can occur, but only if you can get the whole story. This is something you won't get it they feel like it was a bother for you to come and listen.

Try to NEVER go alone to a private interview

I think the most important lesson to learn is to interview with a partner and not alone. If you have to go it alone, try to conduct the interview in a public place and not in the home. When interviewing in the home, even with a partner or team member, can still be dangerous.

When you go into someone's home, you've gone onto their turf. They know where everything is and you don't. Carrying a phone in should you have to call 911 is important. Sit back right now, close your eyes and imagine your idea of a bad guy. Did they look scruffy, unkempt, big, mean, scary, full of tattoos or even worse? One of the hardest things to do is assess or profile the bad guy. The bad guy may look like your wife or father and not the image that comes to mind like you may think of as a bad news stranger. In fact the tattooed guy down the street may be the biggest teddy bear you'll ever meet.

There isn't a good image of the bad guy and that's why it's important to not go alone. You can develop a profile on the person you're interviewing by paying attention to them. What they say, how they say it and by watching their demeanor. The rapport you build and questions you ask with help to determine who you are talking to and how sincere they are about their problem.

Interview—Acceptance & Confidentiality

This is what's you're looking for when you go to your interview and suggestions of things to do to give you the best interview.

- Show respect and concern—go into the interview and leave your beliefs behind. Go in with an open mind and be respectful of their beliefs and customs which may be different than your own beliefs.
- Don't appear moralistic or disapproving—stick with the open mind if you want to get all the information. You may be Christian and they might be Pagan. If this

is someone you don't approve or that disapproval will be felt and it may be better to hand off the client to another investigation team. Chances are that you'll encounter someone who has ways you don't approve of in your life. It's only natural because there are so many different beliefs and customs in the world. Here's where going into the interview unbiased is once again important.

- Remain objective—remaining unbiased continues and allows you to remain objective. If you can't remain objective something may be missed during the interview. An important question may not get asked. Once again, if you think you might have trouble remaining objective then hand off the interview to another team or someone else in your own team. Remaining objective can also pertain to what the client claims to have happened in their home. Instead of going into the interview believing everything the client said over the phone as truth, remain objective so that you'll be able to research other avenues when it comes to what has happened. If you go into the interview 100 percent believing there are important questions you may not ask and clues you might miss.

- Insure confidentiality—how much is made public is the choice of the client. This is one of the most important aspects of working with private clients. It's a cover yourself point, unless you want to possibly get sued one day. Ask the client what they want made public, if anything, and honor that want. By now you should have gained the trust of the client and they will tell you extremely personal information, possibly embarrassing, during the interview. This is how you know there is a good rapport and you're obtaining information to help with the investigation. This trust is sacred to most clients. They may look at you as though they're talking to their doctor or an attorney. They aren't but most are going to expect the same confidentiality. If it's broken, they may get embarrassed, loose a job or worse and even sue for allowing the information to become pubic.

CHAPTER 3

EMPATHY & UNDERSTANDING

Empathy—walk in their shoes and understand how they feel. Take the time to imagine yourself in their place. How would you feel? How hard would it be for you to talk to a stranger about something you don't understand or even believe exists? This can convey warmth; build trust, show interest and respect. By trying to understand how they feel, even if you can't imagine it goes miles toward building trust and rapport. It shows a readiness to help and not send out red flags that you're only looking for an investigation.

Understanding can be key to the investigation. Understanding how they feel gives you a better place to be when asking tough questions. You never know where the questions will lead you or how much they will tell.

ETP received a call from a young female several years ago about a case where she thought demons were involved. The phone interview was bizarre and somewhat brief because it was felt the investigators could get a better "read" on the potential clients in person. There are some things that are difficult to do over the phone for most people. Even those with psychic abilities can at times get a better read on the person when face to face.

The woman talked about her husband trying to kill himself and at the same time his sister, while at a different location, tried to do the same. The caller said her husband would do scary things when he was asleep. His hand would go up in the air and give her the finger or he would get pulled out of bed. She told of receiving a phone call from a caller who later didn't show up in her phone. When she answered the phone a voice told her she needed to, "Get home now." When she arrived she found her husband in the bathroom. He had just tried to hang himself from the shower curtain rod. Then at the same time his sister's boyfriend received the same type of message about her. When he got home, he found her in the bathroom attempting to cut her wrists.

The caller's husband was transported to the hospital for evaluation and released the next day. Since there was verifiable medical history two team members agreed to meet with the husband and wife. They met in a park near where they lived. This was done to help ascertain if there was anything attached to either person. Team members met with them and during the interview were told seriously personal information. The couple wasn't concerned about who else knew the information and the team knew this because they discussed with them how they wanted to proceed with the interview. ETP has a form the client fills out and signs that states nothing is made public, anything can be made public as long as they or the location can be identified or that everything can become public.

This couple wasn't concerned about information getting out in the public. The team has chosen to not identify them or their location because the information was very personal. The interview revealed the husband was male and female. He and his sister were sexually abused by their mother and stepfather, who was serving time in prison in another state. They never revealed their mother as an abuser because they had a younger sister, who is still in the home. The family was raised in the Voodoo religion and was actively practicing their faith. Their mother expected them to take over for her as she aged and to not leave. She was a serious Hoodoo practitioner and taught them her rituals since they were small children. When he and his sister decided to leave home his sister took her bed with her. When she moved it, they discovered a pentagram burned into the wood floor under her bed. Upon seeing this they went into his room, moved the bed and found the same. While he was packing his mother came into the room and said, "I cleaned your brush for you because I know you don't like it to be dirty." He told the team when she said that it scared him because hair is what she normally used in her Hoodoo rituals. The couple believed that his mother may have put a curse or spell on them to cause he and his sister to try and kill themselves.

During the interview, the wife seemed to be most intent on pushing the demon them and her husband was always asleep when he did weird things. So he had no memory of it. She seemed a little too eager to push the demons and he was confused about why he tried to kill himself. He told the team he had no memory of trying to do that and said he would even know how to go about taking a belt and making it into something he could hang himself with much less step off the bathtub and hand there waiting to die. He believed his mother did this as a curse because they left.

It turned out the house she was renting was only a few blocks away so the team decided to drive past the house on the way home to verify some of their statements. They gave the team names, phone numbers and timelines for other events and were cooperative. No demons appeared during the interview and nothing was found on the audio or video recording of the interview. He told them about other possible criminal events and there was concern about the younger sister still with their mother. Everyone moved and the team was unable to make additional contacts with the family. The mother was no longer in Texas and while child protective services may have been called in the state she moved to, it wasn't able to occur without the knowledge of what state she was in at the time.

When you interview someone and children are involved it's important to remember you might have to make a call to police or child protective services. In Texas if you know about possible abuse and don't make a report you could go to jail. The safety of the children should be more important than any investigation.

During the conversation and interview an incident was described that may have happened a long time ago in another state. Information and details were given about the incident, which was a Hoodoo ritual he described as taking place in order to bring a dead baby back to life for a couple. He and his sister were children when this occurred, according to him. While the team is still digging into this it can be difficult to contact a police department about something that may have occurred a long time ago. It's still possible that may happen. The team members conducting the interview were me and Tamra Brickey. She was a former deputy and now the mayor of an East Texas city. Not everything told to us by the couple was put into this book. Some of it is being kept back should anything ever come out of information told to us.

This information is to show how much information you can get from a client once you build a good rapport with them.

CHAPTER 4

NONVERBAL COMMUNICATION

Nonverbal—any perceived message an individual becomes aware of from another other than language written or spoken which conveys an intended meaning to the receiver.

In other word, watch the client to see how they act, look and behave. Brickey is sitting on the couch facing a client and observing them while another team member is sitting nearby taking notes. You can see she has engaged the client and is listening intently to what they have to say. Everyone felt comfortable and after the interview the team decided to conduct an investigation. It turn out that both the grandmother and grandchild are sensitive and see the dead wherever they go. Their home seemed to be a beacon for wandering souls.

I will have to add that this is one place where I seem to have seen a full body apparition before the interview. Brickey and I drove to the address and then continued on to another location in the community to learn more history about the area. As we passed by the house I saw a tall man, over 6 ft. tall standing on the hill by the house and in between two vehicles. When I saw him I said something to Brickey about hoping he doesn't think we're not coming back. My next thought was, why in the heck I would think that when they don't even know what we look like or what I drive.

When we returned and after about an hour of interviewing I came to the question of who lives in the home. She and her grandchild were the only ones living in the home. I asked her if she had a visitor earlier in the day and she said no one had been there. I asked her who was the man I had seen outside by the vehicles and she began to grin. We had talked about her husband earlier and that he had passed a few years ago. I described him to her and told her that he was tall, slightly heavy, was wearing overalls and a straw cowboy hat. She told me to look at the picture on the shelf of him. It was a portrait of his face and sure enough he was wearing the clothes and had I described to her and to Brickey before we came to the house.

Once again, pay attention to your client's nonverbal cues as you never know what you might learn.

CHAPTER 5

PROXEMICS AND WHAT THEY ARE

Use of space—the space between individuals when interacting with others

- Varies by culture—some cultures have very different use of space between others. It's a good idea to find out something about their culture if they come from a different background.

- Best interview distance—5-8 feet. If you've ever watched *48 Hours* or *Cold Justice* on TV or any of a number of true crime shows have you ever noticed the layout of the interview room? It's the same in nearly every law enforcement agency in the country. There is a table and 2-3 plain Jane chairs. A camera is paced somewhere in the room or mounted in the ceiling or wall. When you interview someone, you do nearly the same, but it's usually at their house and not an interrogation room. Even the police interview won't start out accusatory, but an attempt will be made to build rapport and trust. People have their own space and don't like anyone to get into their space, especially a stranger. Sitting the 5-8 feet from someone is a good distance, but you can move in closer as the interview progresses and you feel they are holding back important information. When you pull in closer, place a hand on their knee or a shoulder this indicates to them you care and want to hear what they have to say. Often this is when the criminal is ready to confess. While you're not talking to a criminal, the same techniques work with good, honest individuals.

Kinesics

This covers body language, movement, gestures, posture and facial expressions. These are all the things important to watch while conducting your interview.

Two Postures

Open posture—allows access to the body, shows the client is relaxed and ready to talk. This is what you want and lets you know there is a good rapport built and you're getting good information.

Closed posture—Denies access to the body, such as crossed arms. If this is what you're seeing during your interview, there's a problem. Do they want to talk? Are they talking to you, nut under duress from the rest of the family? Are they lying to you?

Face to face contact

Place of signals and automatic tension—blushing, tics and perspiration. It's important to watch for signals of truth and deception. Do certain questions make them blush, get a noticeable nervous tic or have they started sweating profusely when they were calm and cool minutes before. Take notice of the signals and ask about the response. Find out why they are feeling as they are feeling. Could again, be as simple as embarrassment at answering certain questions. Maybe they haven't told you everything and suddenly you've asked something close to what they have been afraid to tell. If you notice this, you can dig and find out more.

Watch expressions

Such as saying everything is okay, but they are crying. Almost everyone has had an experience like this with someone they know. Ask more questions. See if you can draw them out and tell you what is wrong.

Such as saying they didn't do it but are shaking their head, yes. The same goes for saying something happened but shaking their head, no. The shake can tell more than what's coming out of their mouth. Again, dig deeper and ask them more questions. Find out what's really happening.

CHAPTER 6

CONTROL, WHO'S A LIAR? EYE CONTACT TIPS

Direct eye contact—gives a sense of intimacy and a positive relationship. Most often you will get the direct eye contact from someone telling the truth. However, it's important to remember and individual bent on telling a "story" may act the same because they want you to "trust" them. This can be a manipulating behavior of someone intent on deception. They may want to chat you up, be chums, ask a lot of questions and come on as overly friendly.

Avoid direct eye contact when—asking extremely personal questions as it may increase feelings of shame, fear or guilt.

Eye diversion—when someone is looking up and to the left or right. Do you know which way indicates if they are making up a story or telling the truth. If you think you do, think again. Do you know if they are right or left handed? This is important to know because how and where they look is dependent on which hand is their dominant hand. Even if they are looking in the direction that makes you think they may be less than truthful, that might not be the case. This isn't an exact science and everyone processes thoughts differently. So what is it? It's an indicator and that's about it. Use it as a guide and tool but don't base your entire decision on which way someone looks.

Attending Behavior

- Used to show you care about the client—we discussed this in a previous chapter. It's important to remember. This is paying attention to the client. If they start crying, get them a tissue.

- Important for them to feel listened to and valued—this is where you look at them, pay attention to them and leave your cell phone alone.

- Needs to sense genuine interest which will allow them to be more open—remember, act interested, even if you're not. You may get there and find out there's no merit to their claim. Treat them with respect and then leave in a polite way.

- Be on time—remember detail from previous conversations and emails. Call if you can't make it or if you're going to be late. This is a common courtesy that the client will appreciate and remember. Review your notes before arrival so you can remember why they called and know what questions to ask. It's rather difficult to ask the right questions when you can't remember why your there in the first place.

- Follow through—with all promises. Whatever it is that you say you're going to do, do it.

- Interview location—minimize distractions such as turning off radio, TV, not checking your phone or texting during the interview. It's difficult to interview a client if they're more interested in what's happening on the TV than your questions.

- Eye contact—show them you're interested.

- Relaxed and leaning inward—shows interest. The opposite indicated just that, lack of interest or maybe hiding information.

- Smile—at appropriate times, laugh at others if appropriate.

- Responses to their statements—can convey interest and help keep them talking. It shows you're paying attention to what is being said. Often some of your best questions come after they've given you a statement. It may direct you into another line of questioning. It may bring up activity that wasn't reported during the initial contact.

- Quiet listening—gives them a chance to continue on their own. This is an important and well learned tool. By keeping quiet while the client is talking and allowing them to complete their statement without interruptions keeps them on tract to answer the question. Then by keeping quiet once they stop talking gives them the opportunity to continue to think about what was said. Many times they will continue to talk given the opportunity and you might obtain additional information that that's critical to the case. Act like a negotiator. To be a good negotiator you must be a good listener.

CHAPTER 7

CORROBORATION, HISTORY, LINKS AND QUESTIONS

Corroborate their story if possible. This is important to learning whether there is anything to their claims. There are many ways to do this other than taking their story as the only place of information. This can put your mind at ease that the client is truthful and what they describe as happening is happening. It can also give you ideas about who or what could have caused the activity. It may even help you to ease the minds of the client. Below is a list of things that can be done to help.

- Link events and people when possible—see if you can get them to keep a journal and maybe you can put together a timeline of events. Talk to others, research history of the location and anything that happened near there through the years.

- Ask specific—names, times and dates. It's needed and important in order to corroborate their statements. It gives you times, places and people to check with to help give their statements credibility. If they are hesitant to give you this information, it might be an indicator that something might not be as it seems. Maybe nothing is really happening and their looking for fun or 15 minutes of fame.

• Contact other witnesses—when you get the names of witnesses try to get contact information so you can either call them or interview them face to face.

• Talk to the neighbors—this can be as simple as knocking on their door and asking them how long they've lived there. If they've lived there a long time you may be able to find out about other individuals who have lived in the home. Ask questions that aren't leading but open ended without giving them any information. You client may not want the neighbor to know they think something paranormal is happening in their home. You can ask the neighbor if they've heard or seen anything unusual at the house while living next door. Be sure to watch their expressions as you ask the questions. It may help you know if they know something or not.

• Talk to former owners—talk to them the same way you would talk to the neighbor.

• Religious beliefs—ask the client about their religious beliefs. This may play a role in what they perceive is happening in their home. It may be a reason they don't want their family or friends to know what's happening. But then again, they may have a good support system within their church congregation.

- Criminal history—have they been arrested? Some think it's not important to know if the client has ever been arrested or why. While it may not always be important, it could play a part as to the credibility of the client. Say they were arrested several times for drugs but say when activity occurs they aren't on drugs. In reality, that may or may not be the case. If they were arrested for fraudulent activities are they telling you the truth about the paranormal activity or do they see it as a possible way to make a buck? The list goes on and can really give you a good indication of who your client is as an individual.

- Social history—where they come from, family life, any abusive situations? This can be a big tell as well and important when it comes to helping the family. Does what they think is happening have anything to do with outside factor that are not paranormal? By asking these difficult questions you will learn a lot about your client and be better able to help point them in the right direction.

- Work—what do they do? Whether or not they are currently working isn't important. What is important is to know what kind of work they do, where and any interesting work history. This could play a part on the investigation. Is there stress, are they worried about their job and not sleeping well?

- Medical and Mental history—and a diagnosis. Again, this can be very important. Be sure to ask the questions about their mental state and health. If they are Bi-polar it doesn't mean run from the house because they're imagining the activity. If they have a heart condition or any other mental health or physical problem you may want to require certain things before considering an investigation. You are a responsible person and should someone perceive you cause a person with problems to get worse, you could get sued. A good question to ask someone with a mental problem is if they hear voices. If the answer is yes, ask if they are hearing voices while you are there. If the answer is yes, be sure to ask them what the voices are telling them to do. This is important. Every so often we hear in the news where someone has butchered or tortured their child to death because the child was a demon or God was telling them they had to do this. At this point, if the client is hearing voices you may insist they get a mental and medical evaluation before you will consider conducting an evaluation. It's in the best interest of both parties. You can be held responsible if something were to go south after you left.

- Drugs—do they use drugs? Good to know.

- Drink—how much, what and when? This is also good to know.

CHAPTER 8

PARANORMAL BELIEFS

Do they watch paranormal shows? A question that should be asked in the beginning, possibly on the phone before the interview gets to the in person stage. ETP has learned that some of the cases which come across as sounding the most serious often come from those who watch every paranormal show they can find on TV. The only experience they have is what they see on TV. Most people believe everything in all the paranormal shows are 100 percent the truth. The idea that something in the shows might not be accurate is beyond their belief. To think it could be scripted and some of the evidence might not be real evidence shocks them to learn.

Many people who watch all the shows seem to jump to the conclusion when something happens in their house it has to be paranormal. This includes sounds of the house settling, branches scraping against the house in the wind or doors which seem to open or close on their own. Many of these events can be explained to the client in a rational way by the interviewer. If necessary you can take the client to the problem areas and show them how it's not paranormal but perfectly normal. They could live in an area where sound travels far, like on a lake, and they could hear voices drifting over the water from miles away at night.

ETP took a call from a woman who sounded upset while on the phone. She and her husband just merged their family and they had eight children ranging in ages from about two to 14. She said that there was activity in the house before she and her children moved in and it had seemed rather benign at first. She said a spirit or imaginary friend had been with her husband most of his life and whenever her husband moved throughout his life he would invite his "friend" to come with him. His children were used to the friend who could be heard wandering about the house by way of footsteps. Then she and her children moved in turning the smaller family into one much larger. Most of the children slept upstairs. She said when they started cleaning out the send floor for the children to move into activity seemed to ramp up and it was scaring the children.

ETP moved quickly and went to the house for an interview and small investigation because children were involved. When they got there two team members interviewed the parents while two other members, myself included, interviewed the eight children. As you can imagine it was rather hectic trying to interview all the children. They claimed closet doors opened on their own and voices could be heard talking to a few of the children in a threatening manner.

Nothing was picked up on audio or video by ETP while interviewing the family.

Instead what the team found was while dad did have something going on and it had been there all his life and wasn't threatening. While talking with the children we learned they had talked a lot among themselves about paranormal activity and all the children seemed to have had a steady dose of scary and paranormal movies. One child claimed he was pulled out of his bed by the leg and then it was learned he had seen all the *Paranormal Activity* movies as had the rest of the siblings. ETP conducted a small investigation, knowing that the claims were probably due to over active imaginations after talking with the children. The investigation fascinated the children and seemed to calm them down like a sugar pill might do for a sick person. The family was contacted a few more times and everything was calm at the house and back to normal with no complaints. ETP suggested the parents watch what their children are allowed to view on TV and maybe include more age appropriate movies and TV. So be sure to ask if they watch paranormal shows.

What do they believe? Not only ask if they watch paranormal shows but ask this question. It helps understand where they're coming from when they call to ask for help. If you have a skeptic on your hands and they are calling for help it may make you think something may really be there causing trouble. Skeptics can have a hard time calling to ask for help because they don't believe any of it is real. Sometimes they end up believers when it does happen to them. If you are a skeptical believer it's possible you could remain more objective during the interview than someone looking to prove what is said is paranormal. Someone could do this during an interview if the client is a true believer. It could even lead the team to move in a different way.

ETP had a call from a woman who was a paramedic and a member of a paranormal team. Most people would think she knew what she was talking about when she called. She and her husband were having marital problems and thought maybe the activity was the cause. She claimed her team had conducted an investigation of her home without finding any evidence. She thought the house was a bad place and she was better when she was not in the house. ETP agreed to conduct an investigation. When several team members arrived, including myself, she was nowhere to be found. It seemed no one was home and she wouldn't answer the phone. As they are about to drive off the husband comes outside from the back door and wants to know what's going on.

It turned out that she forget to tell him ETP was coming and she wasn't even staying at the house. He called her from a different number and she came to the home. They were interviewed and a small investigation took place. After talking to them ETP felt while there could be something there, the problem was pretty much between the couple. If there was anything at the house, it wasn't evil, but could be feeding off their negativity when they fought. After more discussion it was learned that a man who was abusive toward his wife met an untimely death in the house. The house was old and pre-civil war. Who knows who lived there and what happened through the years. ETP was told that the previous home owner was very abusive and was in the middle of a domestic violence episode when he fell out the back door and down the stairs to his death.

What was possible was that the "accident" may not be as it was told and he could be around the house and angry that he's dead. It's possible that since he was, allegedly an angry and abusive person the negativity in the house is being picked up by household members and getting projected into their relationship. The woman said she feels different when she's away from the house and that her husband's personality changed when they moved into the house. The suggestion to them was to fill the house with love and light and to see a marriage counselor if they wanted to try and keep the marriage together. This was a first for ETP—suggesting marriage counseling.

What do they think is in their house or following them? This is a good question to ask.

Occult practices? It's important to know if they practice any occult activity or if it has occurred in their home or on their property.

Ouija board, séances or anything else of this nature? Something else to ask, especially if there are teens in the home. It's possible something came through that doesn't belong. While asking questions you can help educate them about things that can go wrong. A good example is what happened recently when ETP, myself included, assisted another team with an investigation. There were a number of children and teens at the home. While they think something is happening in their home and it was scaring them. It was also learned that there are two houses down the street the children go to almost daily for thrills. The two homes are old and abandoned. All of them described a heavy feeling when on the property. We explained before leaving that maybe they shouldn't go to this property should something be there. It could be possible something might come home with them. Turned out nobody had thought about that happening. You can never ask too many questions.

Magic—ask if they believe in magic, Voodoo, Santeria, or anything else like this or if they are practitioners.

CHAPTER 9

HOW TO INTERVIEW ANYONE—LET THEM TELL THEIR STORY

Listen—nothing else needs to get said about this statement.

- Take notes—bring your notebook along to take notes while a second person asked questions. When you think you're done go off together and review everything for a few minutes to make sure you didn't miss something. If possible record the interview with audio and video.

- Go over what they say to make sure you understand what they said—that is, go over it with the client. While going over what they said you can ask additional questions, clarify a point and the client might even think of additional information.

- Then ask more questions. You can never ask too many questions.

- Go over the statement one more time if possible and fill in all the detail. Leave no stone unturned. Leave the house with all the information you'll need to go over with the rest of the team and to conduct research.

- Ask them to define broad statements. You've heard others describe things by saying something like, "He cussed at me," or "He is mean." Get more information from them. Ask them to describe what happened without generalizing. For example, when the client said he was cussing, ask what was said. If the client said someone was mean, ask what they were doing that makes them mean. If you were talking to a child their description could include they were mean because he doesn't let me do what I want or he makes me clean up my room. Everyone has a different idea or interpretation of broad statements. Once I interviewed an elderly lady for a criminal report and she described the suspect as a young boy. She was in her eighties and when asked about what age I was thinking teen until she said he was about 40-50 years old. Please don't assume you know what they mean.

Research Information

- Check local newspapers for past information about anything that may have occurred on or near the property. This can include deaths, arrests, fires or any other kind of tragedy.

- Check with the historical society and commission. You can find a plethora of information at their locations. You can search through their files for old photographs, obituaries, letters and so much more that might help tie in with claims of activity on the property.

- Check with law enforcement for any reports. In many states this information is public record once a case is closed. Simply fill out a public information request for anything that may have happened at a specific address. It may take 10-20 days to get a response and it could cost a small amount of money. That depends on the municipality and how long it will take to retrieve any information. Also it will depend on what actions are needed to fill the request, whether it can be done on the computer or has to get done manually.

- Check local cemetery for names of former occupants. Check with the county or district court clerk for deeds of the property. The deeds will have the names of former owners.

- Talk to family members, neighbors and friends.

CHAPTER 10

THINGS MAY NOT BE AS THEY SEEM

Really there?

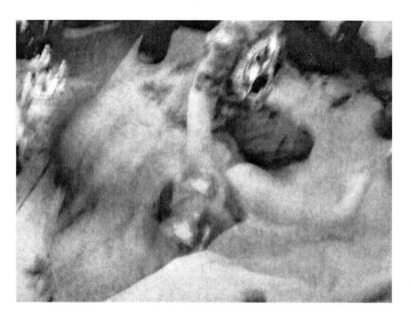

    I received the photograph from a client several years ago. She gave it to me and would have given me the negative if she could have found it. The photograph was taken with an older model 35mm point and shoot camera. I talked about the client in one of the chapters before this chapter. I cropped the photo so nothing shows the identity of her or her family. She took the photo during a Christmas holiday and many family members were present. Take a good look at the picture. Near the bottom of the photo you can see legs extending from a seated position. Superimposed over the person in a chair is the blurred individual smiling and looking at the camera. She didn't want the picture at her house any more. When her family saw the photo it scared them and now most of the family won't come to her house. The blurred smiling person with the dark hair was not in the room and none of the family members recognize the child. Wells Fargo ran their stagecoach service from the community she lives in as a stop on the way to Dallas during the 1800's. She said there's been activity outside because the stagecoach ran right through the back of her property.

I have no idea what happened in the photo and how it came to be. She didn't have a clue as to how to do this and she had it developed at a commercial lab from a big box store. It wasn't a double exposure from her camera. It didn't have the capabilities to take double exposures. The photo is a good example of, "What is it?"

Here is another example of, "Is it as it seems?" Brickey and I were conducting an interview when a woman brought out her Bible and told us she woke up in the morning and discovered her Bible was not in her bed but was on the floor and on the other side of the room. We took a look at the Bible and torn pages. When examining them closely we were able to see finger indentions from the individual who really tore the pages out of the Bible. It was a human and not a spirit or demon. There is more detail about this in an upcoming chapter.

CHAPTER 11

WHAT TO TAKE TO AN INTERVIEW

- Paper and pen—to take notes. Also bring your questions. There is a list of questions asked by ETP in an upcoming chapter. Bring more than you need. Yu could even end up asking individuals to write down their experiences if there are a lot of people to interview. At the least bring pen and paper for yourself. Be sure to bring more than one pen so you don't have to scramble to find a pen should yours run out of ink or break.

- Voice recorder—to pick up any electronic voice phenomenon (EVP) or in case you forget what was said or your pen breaks. It's good to record the interview and refresh your memory before going to conduct an investigation. It's possible the client might change their story when you arrive for the investigation. If the story is not completely factual you will have the recorded interview to go back to for clarification.

- Video recorder—used to review client's body clues and check for anything not seen or heard. It's another tool that can pick up an EVP. If you get the same sounds on audio and video, you just might have something.

It can also help you discover anything not paranormal causing something to happen within it's line of sight.

- Camera—if returning to see how everything looks to compare for changes. You can go over the photographs taken during the interview to see if something doesn't look right. Then if you go back for an investigation you can try to recreate what you shot during the interview. You can also go back and check what something is that may look unusual in one of the photos. Have you ever gone over photographs after returning home from an investigation only to discover something doesn't look right? Then you call the client back and ask them about the photo. You ask what was in the room or what was sitting on a piece of furniture. Then there are the times you have to go back and see for yourself. If photos are taken during the interview of the property it will give you something to be aware of before going into the investigation.

- Electro Magnetic Field (EMF) for base readings—to use for the investigation. If you get base readings while snapping photographs during the interview once again you'll have something to go by when you return for the investigation. Should readings be quite different in a certain spot on one of the visits, it may prompt you to search for reasons why it's different.

- A waiver—for the client to sign. The waiver is for the protection of the client and the team. This is what the client signs and decides what can and can't be made public.

CHAPTER 12

FAKE OR REAL?

There has been much discussion amongst the paranormal community about fakers and fraud. Teams have been sued by other teams or team members. Then there are those teams touting the why can't we all be friends and share with each other while lambasting other teams and individuals in the same breath. This chapter is about the fact that it might be a good thing to be somewhat skeptical when talking to an individual about possible activity in their home, public place or business.

Anyone interested in what the paranormal community is saying about fakes or scams just has to Google paranormal fraud and they will come up with nearly 6,000,000 results in seconds. There are individuals calling themselves doctors, who aren't doctors, ministers who aren't ministers and demonologist who have no training. In many states all you have to do is use the word doctor and have others believe you are a doctor to commit a felony. Others may hold themselves to be inventors of equipment that can be applied to the paranormal field, but not really be the inventor of anything. There are some good and trusted inventors of cool paranormal gadgets to be found. Just be sure to do your due diligence before purchasing anything from someone you don't know. Ask around the paranormal community for information about a product or seller. Get several opinions before spending a lot of money. When the true scientists and researchers within the paranormal realm begin asking too many questions some of these individual fakers will begin to fade away. There is an interesting article on About.com, *"Burden of Proof"* that discusses where the burden lies, with the skeptic or the believers. While this may not cover fakers and fraud, the information does apply to this as well. But then there are some even worse.

They are real criminals and should be charged with a criminal offense. A recent conversation with another investigator centered on a paranormal group that was new and turned out to be not so interested in the paranormal. When they were contacted by individuals with questions or asking for help they would set up an investigation time the same as most groups. They would arrive at the home without plans to do an investigation. When they made contact with the homeowner they had the stipulation that they would not conduct any investigation with the homeowner present. Once the homeowner left, they would steal items from the home and the homeowner would return to their home to find valuable items missing from where they belonged. Most people would think this couldn't last too long as it would be fairly easy to track them down. That is if they use their real names and so on and if the homeowner was not too embarrassed to make a report. It's a good idea for the individual contacting a group to be sure and take some time to do their due diligence search on the group and maybe even the founder. Most groups are legitimate and won't be offended if the caller asks questions or even for references. After all, it is their home and they are asking strangers to come for the evening.

One woman decided she had demons in her home. She set out to find the quickest way she could find to get rid of them. She contacted ETP and we responded quickly because she has a child in the home. The photograph above is what they found on the 11 year old child's door when they arrived for the interview. Another of the woman's Bible can be found in an earlier chapter. I took her frantic call and listened to her hysterical talk. I calmed her down and when I said it would be okay until we could get there over the weekend she suddenly decided she had been injured by a creature and had a bruise to prove it. She sent a couple photos but it was possible she caused the bruising to make it seem worse than it was when she called. Each time I mentioned something wasn't happening she suddenly remembered that it did happen to her. It was a case where I didn't know if we would end up making a child protective service call or not when we left. Brickey and I went to the apartment for the interview. We were told activity picked up the night she followed some instructions she received in the mail. The instructions were to use anointing oil in various places around the home, say certain prayers, and write something on a piece of paper and sleep with it under her pillow. Then the first thing she was to do the following morning was to put the paper, along with money, into an envelope and mail so the person receiving it could pray for them and make everything go away. We advised this was a scam and to not send any money to person in the flyer. We arranged to conduct an investigation several days later. Before the investigation, she called me and explained she had two men come to the house, but wasn't able to explain where she found them. They had come to cleanse her house, telling her not to have ETP come over and conduct an investigation. While the two unknown men were at the residence, so was the woman's daughter. The men started their cleansing and put oils on a variety of places within the home. Then they had the woman in her bedroom and told her to disrobe so they could "cleanse" her. They said this would have applied to her daughter if she was 12, she was 11. The scary part is what might have happened, if her daughter had not been present. The woman refused to disrobe. Then the men demanded money for their so called "free" home cleansing. She said she got scared but did not have any money and promised to send them some in a few days and they left. She told me she was still going to send them money because she promised she would send it. We counseled her about scam artists and the dangers of allowing just anyone into her home. It was such a concern we tried to get information from her regarding the men because we wanted to report this to police. She didn't want to give out the information.

ETP conducted the investigation and nothing was found. The family watched every paranormal show on TV. Her daughter had a vivid imagination and grandpa was a preacher. The woman talked about a lot of activity occurring in her daughter's bedroom. There were two closets in the room. One had the electric box for the apartment in it and had a high EMF reading. The other closet had an even higher EMF reading when the woman's TV was on in her bedroom. The back of the TV was touching the back of the closet wall. They lived in an older apartment complex that hadn't been updated, if ever, in many years. There was a single light bulb socket hanging by old wiring dangling in her daughter's bedroom. One of the complaints was that the light bulb in the socket in that room would blow each and every time they put in a bulb. We suggested she was putting in too strong of a bulb and that would cause it to blow. She mentioned a creature crawling up and down the wall in the hallway she could only see when in the bathroom. Headlights caused light anomalies in the hallway. She said the maintenance man had been at the apartment on calls for service 27 times and the last time he was in the closet and the door shut and locked on him. There was no lock on the door. What she really wanted was to be able to tell the landlord the apartment was haunted so she could get out of her lease. When we wouldn't say that she got mad at us. Then a year or two later she called with the exact same story about her apartment in another city. I told her we wouldn't be coming to the apartment to help her get out of her lease. We haven't heard from her since.

This can cause all kinds of problems from a real situation getting worse along with even more distrust of the paranormal community in general. While the paranormal community may not ever get rid of the fakers by working together cohesively they may make a dent and help the scientific community one day accept more of the data.

There are pages on Facebook and Twitter with missions to expose fraud. These can be good places to obtain current data about information you may not know regarding current scamming trends. But then some are put together by bullies under false pretense that thrive on hating or spreading lies about individuals and groups within the community they don't even know. Those victimized usually want to reply and clear their name. The best thing they or you can do is to ignore them. They are looking for the conflict. It's hard to do and some really nice, honest hard working people have been hurt or even left the paranormal community as a result. They were making good progress in helping people and it's a shame they chose to move on. Drama won't help anyone in the community and has no place, but just like Peyton Place, is something that will always be around. Just like it is important to remember when watching TV paranormal shows that they are for entertainment purposes only as are many paranormal phone applications. They are not always the best place to learn how to conduct a proper paranormal investigation just like some of the TV police shows are not the place to learn how to be a good officer. Individuals who are interested in the paranormal field should try to connect with some good and experienced paranormal researchers, groups or investigators willing to take the time to mentor. By taking the time to do this the experienced will help educate and alleviate some of the misconceptions in the field. The experienced might consider themselves the village and take it from there, which is better than creating the Paranormal Police.

- There are several important things to remember when talking with or locating someone to help you with possible unexplained activity in your home:
- There is no such thing as a guaranteed removal of activity. It's not like buying that guaranteed used car. The science is not exact.
- The group you call should not charge a penny to help. If they do, beware and call another group. Now if they're in FL and you are asking them to come to CO they may ask for travel expenses. Most people conduct paranormal investigations as a service to the public and spend their own hard earned money for equipment and the time it takes to travel, investigate and review their finding.
- Ask how long they have been around and what kind of experience members in the group have with the paranormal. Legitimate groups won't be offended.
- If an individual used doctor in their name ask where they went to school.
- If a group requires you to leave your home and you don't want to, don't. An honest group will probably want you nearby in case they have questions during their investigation. Be suspicious if they say they will only come if you leave.
- Most groups will ask you to sign a release. That's standard practice. Remember it is your house and you do not have to have the information released to the public. Most legitimate groups give the homeowner the choice to decide how much if anything is made public.

A recent conversation with an investigator was about how a location asked them to come and investigation. Prior to the investigation the location was researched to determine if there was any sort of a past that could cause unexplained activity and there was none. The house while brand new was made to appear to be very old. The group went in and was able to determine that the owners had set up the house so it appeared to be active when it was not. Investigators should be prepared to look for scams on the other end as well.

CHAPTER 13

ORBS, DUST OR REFLECTIONS—WHICH IS IT?

Orbs, Dust or Reflections—Which is it? Now this is the question investigators and researchers would really like to know. There are many opinions regarding orbs and discussions have even turned ugly between believers and skeptics. Do you know where you stand on the subject? This seems to be a difficult question to answer and beliefs are usually strong as to what makes an orb. The skeptic's response may come across more plausible than that of a believer.

ETP posted an *Orbs Debunked* article by Troy Taylor on their website, etxhaunted.com, in an effort to help educate those interested in the paranormal and orbs. Taylor takes the stance of many researchers and skeptics within this community. Orb photographs are taken of many things which can include dust, light reflections in the lens, dirt, pollen and so on. Why does it seem to happen in so many declared haunted locations? It does but happens in many other places as well. A possible explanation could be that many of these locations are old dusty buildings, maybe a crowded home full of dust or are at outside locations such as cemeteries. Does the location have to be declared haunted to take the so called orb photograph? Most definitely not since the same conditions occur in a myriad of locations. There are many books written about photography and ghosts. Taylor's *Ghosts on Film* from the Haunted Field Guide Series is one example.

There was a discussion in a paranormal group regarding orbs. Some of the participants warned individuals they would probably get "slammed" if questions were asked but one person was braved and asked away. While the discussion became heated, it was a good exchange of ideas and beliefs where one could say everyone agreed to disagree. Such discussions can be a good thing as it helps educate.

Orbs are not something to bring to the scientific community if an individual expects to be taken seriously as a researcher within that community. Then again, everyone learned during their school years that most of what we know or use, such as electricity or even that the world is round, came from the scientist or researcher, who was laughed out of the scientific community. Skeptics with closed minds can stifle growth and discoveries while the open minded skeptic can be good to have around.

There are many extremely intelligent individuals studying the paranormal. Conversations with them can be mind stimulating and possibly even lead to a new discovery when groups talk instead of shut down communication. YouTube has many orb videos. Most of them are videos of, "look at the orbs I captured" and some will try to sway the skeptic into their way of thinking. A video done by one group could fall under this classification. On the video the individual attempts to show skeptics that orbs are ghosts or spiritual and intelligent beings. He claims to be in the rooms alone and even stomps on the carpet in an attempt to make orbs for the camera. He gets comfy on the bed after stomping about and shows through panning his video that no orbs are floating around the room so that is probably not what causes orbs. He shows more in the video where orbs show up in the room on demand in the area of the room where he asks the spirit to appear. He's very polite as he is telling the "orb" where to show itself. The "orb" in the video is suspicious if not only for the fact that there is no video showing what he is doing at the time or if indeed he is alone in the room. He does comment that a skeptic will probably see the orbs and say they were made by a flashlight. A better video of his experiment if it was done as stated would have been to have the entire room captured on video to show nothing has been staged. Otherwise it just appears to be non-paranormal, even if the person is well respected in the field. Full disclosure helps.

Orbs were rarely seen before the invention of digital cameras. In the beginning there were orbs everywhere. Most of that has to do with the megapixels in the camera. The optics of the lens and many other features. I have a Canon EOS 60 D and rarely do I find an "orb" in my photos. You will still find them in the lower end cameras, even if the megapixels are high.

There are some paranormal researchers who believe, like many, that there are true orbs that can be seen with your eyes and this is what determines it is an orb.

Some of the true orb believers say orbs are beings, spirits, ghosts or energy and not mainly dust and particulates. paulcmuir created Hopi Mythology, Tree Spirits and Orbs, a video that can be seen on YouTube regarding the study into the Orb Bar Wave. They show comparison images between fibroblasts, division, rock art, orbs and creation energy in their study data. The video shows a wide variety of images and how similar they are when viewed. The images are interesting and could lead to quite the discussion between believers and skeptics.

Ghostweb.com posted an article or statement on orbs and states that dust is the most common anomaly photographed by the beginning ghost investigator. They suggest a new investigator shoot about 100 photos of dust, pollen, spores, rain, etc. to see what they look like and to establish a baseline for later comparison. Ghostweb.com explains the term orb was coined in 1994 as a term to cover all of the anomalies found while taking photos and was not meant to mean ghosts.

It seems the jury is still out as to what orbs may or may not be energy or dust? That is a question which may never be answered, at least not for many years. Just Google orbs and there will be thousands of sites to read in an attempt to decide what an orb is. You may come away more confused than ever but knowledge is always power so search away.

CHAPTER 14

HOW DO WE KNOW WHAT IS A GHOST? ARE THEY PARANORMAL?

How do we know what is a ghost? Are they paranormal? This is a question that has most likely been asked for hundreds if not thousands of years. There are many different beliefs that can be found in a myriad of cultures. Some cultures view ghosts as a bad thing while others embrace ghosts. Many books have been written about ghosts from quite a few different viewpoints.

This discussion may last as long as humans can communicate or maybe one day the discussion will be settled with a definitive answer. There are vast numbers of individuals seeking such answers through research even though some individuals believe they already know the answer. For many the answers come from their culture or faith and believe as they do because this is what they were taught. Some thoughts have been that ghosts are not really ghosts but beings in another dimension and possibly a worm hole of sorts briefly opened and those beings or a look into that dimension becomes possible. Some may even think ghosts are not ghosts but beings from outer space. Then there are those too afraid to even discuss the thought of ghosts because their faith has taught them that all ghost are evil, occult and of the devil.

ETP once had a case they shared with another group due to distance. This was a good case of paranormal unity between groups that led to some help for a family who had never thought of the possibility of dealing with the unknown. Their entire family is Church of Christ and *Sally (name of the client was changed to protect her and her family)* called in frantic need of help not knowing what to do because what she claimed was happening to her family was shaking their belief system to its core. Some of the family members were so stringent in their beliefs that they think Catholics are still going to hell. Sally was advised she was talking to someone of the Catholic faith and that was fine by her, but she would not tell her family. Her claim was that something was attacking her young son and following him everywhere. She said doors would open and close for him as he entered and left a room. She said furniture would be moved around in him room and even in an entire house. He, we'll call him Jason, went to stay with other family members during this time and Sally said it followed him there and now other family members were involved and witnessing strange events. Sally called and wanted immediate relief over the phone and to know what was happening. She learned that it doesn't happen that way and someone could come to her home to help. ETP contacted a group that was closer to help and help they did. Things quieted down around the households after several visits from the paranormal group. What was there? ETP and the other group are not sure, neither is Sally. Did it shake her families' beliefs? You bet it did. They are still strong in their faith but was it a ghost? That is still unknown. Are there unexplained events occurring in the house? Yes they are and both groups are still in contact with Sally and will remain that way as long as needed. Eventually ETP and the other group backed off from helping the family. It was dysfunctional and there was trouble with them following through on suggestions made to help.

Now, back to the main topic of what is a ghost. A search on Google will give you 457,000,000 results you can go through and read from now until the day you die. Many are fascinating while others seem just plain crazy. The difficult task would be learning to discern what is legitimate and what is not.

According to one entry in Wikipedia a ghost is described as, "In traditional belief and fiction, a ghost is the soul or spirit of a deceased person or animal that can appear, in visible form or other manifestation, to the living. Descriptions of the apparition of ghosts vary widely from an invisible presence to translucent or barely visible wispy shapes, to realistic, life-like visions. The deliberate attempt to contact the spirit of a deceased person is known as necromancy, or in spiritism as a *séance*. The belief in manifestations of the spirits of the dead is widespread, dating back to animism or ancestor worship in pre-literate cultures. Certain religious practices—funeral rites, exorcisms, and some practices of spiritualism and ritual magic—are specifically designed to appease the spirits of the dead. Ghosts are generally described as solitary essences that haunt particular locations, objects, or people they were associated with in life, though stories of the phantom armies, ghost trains, phantom ships, and even ghost animals have also been recounted."

Merrian-Webster describes ghost as, ": the seat of life or intelligence: soul <give up the *ghost*>
2: a disembodied soul; *especially*: the soul of a dead person believed to be an inhabitant of the unseen world or to appear to the living in bodily likeness
3: spirit, demon

4*a* : a faint shadowy trace <a *ghost* of a smile> *b* : the least bit <not a *ghost* of a chance>

5: a false image in a photographic negative or on a television screen caused especially by reflection

6: one who ghostwrites

7: a red blood cell that has lost its hemoglobin

—ghost·like *adjective*

—ghosty *adjective*"

About.com has a description under Paranormal Phenomena that describes a ghost as, "A ghost—or spirit or apparition—is the energy, soul or personality of a person who has died and has somehow gotten stuck between this plane of existence and the next. Most researchers believe that these spirits do not know they are dead. Very often they have died under traumatic, unusual or highly emotional circumstances. Ghosts can be perceived by the living in a number of ways: through sight (apparitions), sound (voices), smell (fragrances and odors), touch—and sometimes they can just be sensed."

CHAPTER 15

FORENSIC KIT EXTREME

This forensic kit information was provided by David Rountree, author of 'Paranormal Technology'. It's quite comprehensive for most individuals, but it does give a good example of items that can be used during interviews, walk-throughs and investigations to help determine if it's paranormal or not.

FINGERPRINT EQUIPMENT:
- Brushes:
    - Fiberglass (3)
    - Camel Hair (2)
    - Magnetic Wand
    - Wide Magnetic Wand
- Powders:
    - Black (regular and magna)
    - Silver (regular and magna)
    - Redwop Lift
- Tape:(must be compatible to powder and cards)
    - 2" Wide
    - 4" Wide
    - Rubber Tape
- Lift Cards:(must be compatible to powder and tape)

- Black
- White
- Regular size and 8" by 12" in both colors
- Magnifying Glass

CASTING EQUIPMENT:
- Plaster of Paris (5 lbs)
- Dental Powder (2 gallons)
- Silicone casting material
- Dupli-cast
- Mikrosil Rubber
- Mixing Bowl (2 sizes)
- Rubber Spatula
- Reinforcement mesh
- Plastic Bags
- Metal Retaining Ring
- Plastic Weigh Boats
- Wooden Tongue Depressors
- Modeling Clay (for dam)
- Identification Tags with string
- Snow wax (for impressions in snow)

PHOTOGRAHIC EQUIPMENT:
Cameras:
- 35mm with adjustable controls
- Digital with adjustable controls
- 2 1/4 with adjustable controls or larger format
- Extra batteries for cameras
- Lens:
- Normal
- Wide angle (28mm maximum)

- Macro (capable of 1:1 ratio)
- Telephoto
- Film:
- Color
- Black and White
- Adequate supply for both formats

Flash:
- Compatible strobes for cameras
- Batteries
- PC cord (6-10 ft.)

Tripod:
- Adjustable head and legs

Measuring Devices:
- Disposable rulers

Filters:
- 80b filter
- Orange filter
- Polarizing
- Miscellaneous
- Lens brush and lens tissue
- Photo flood light
- Camera carrying cases
- Shutter release cable

EVIDENCE PACKAGING SUPPLIES:
- Paper Bags:
- Paper:
- Metal cans:
- Arson debris
- Hands
- Glass Vials
- Evidence Tape

- Marking Pen
- Stapler
- Pill boxes (folding)

BLOOD COLLECTION SUPPLIES:
- Sterilized Cloth Squares
- Sterilized Thread
- Glass Microscope plates
- Distilled Water
- Scalpel
- Disposable Scalpel Blades
- Tweezers (6 assorted pairs)
- Small Scissors
- Luminol

DECEASED PRINT KIT:
- 2" Roller
- 4" Roller
- Black ink
- Porelon pad
- Finger strips
- Plain paper
- Ink remover
- Tissue builder

HAND TOOLS:
- Claw Hammer
- Hack Saw
- Assorted Screwdrivers
- Assorted Pliers
- Pipe Wrench
- Pry bar

- Vise grips
- Wire Cutters
- Bolt Cutters
- Socket Set (metric and standard)
- Wood Chisels
- Hand Axe
- Shovels
- Sifters
- Slim Jim
- Automobile Door Handle Remover
- Pocket Knife
- Leatherman
- Small Leatherman
- Exacto Knife Set

MEASURING DEVICES:
- 12ft Steel Tape
- 26ft Steel Tape
- 100ft Tape
- Laser Measurement Tool

BIOHAZARD KIT
- Disposable latex gloves
- Disposable footwear protectors (booties)
- Disposable face mask/shield
- Disposable gown/apron
- Disposable Bio-Hazardous waste bag (trash)

MISCELLANEOUS EQUIPMENT:
- Flashlight and spare batteries
- Writing paper and report forms
- Graph paper

- Clipboard
- Writing and marking pens
- Pencils
- Sharpies
- Metal scribe
- Dental Tools
- Chalk and crayons
- Cellophane tape and dispenser
- Clear book binding tape
- Extra evidence tape
- Extra staples and stapler
- Scotch Tape
- Scissors
- Large and small forceps
- Hemostats
- Compass
- Large Magnet
- 100ft Nylon rope
- 100ft Electrical Cord
- Metal detector
- Ultra-violet light: Low and high wavelength
- Protective eyewear
- Static lifter
- Portable Laser or Alternate Light Source
- Calculator
- String
- Various size clamps
- Velcro Ties
- Pocket Notebooks
- Bic Lighter
- Glue Stick
- Super Glue

CHAPTER 16

QUESTIONS TO ASK DURING THE INTERVIEW

What follows is a version of the questions used by ETP during our in depth interviews. You can add more questions or move them around to suit your situation, but this should give you a good idea of the kinds of questions to ask.

Name and age:

Home phone:

Cell phone:

Address:

E-Mail Address:

Has any other group or organization been contacted? (If yes, please state who):

How many people live there?

Please list each individual living or working at site with their complete name and age

What do they do for a living?

What are their religious beliefs?

Amount of time at the site or residence?

Age of site?

How many previous owners?

History of the site: (Tragedies, Deaths, Previous Complaints)

How many rooms are at the site?

List each room and what floor it is on, including bathrooms

Also include if basement if finished or not and the attic

Has the site been blessed?

Has there been any recent remodeling?

What remodeling has been done?

Are any occupants on medication?

If yes, what is the medication being used to treat?

What is your highest level of education?

Has anyone ever been arrested? What for?

Anyone interested in the Occult?

Use or used an Ouija Board?

Interested in Séances, Psychics, Witchcraft or Spells?

Please explain your answer in detail if you have answered "Yes":

Does anyone watch paranormal shows or have an interest in the paranormal?

What knowledge and to what extent is your knowledge of the Paranormal?

Which individual, if any, are currently seeing a mental health professional?

Does anyone have trouble sleeping?

Have you are anyone close had a near death experience?

Has anyone close to you passed away recently?

Who, When, and what relationship did you have with the person(s)?

How would the phenomena be explained when you were a child?

What do you believe to be the source of the phenomena and what makes you believe this?

Do you believe in Ghosts, Spirits, or Entities?

If so, how long have you believed in the paranormal?

Do you feel this is threatening? If yes...Who and why do they feel it is?

Have there been any problems with electrical appliances?

What have the problems been?

Have there been any problems with plumbing?

What have the problems been?

Do your electrical devices plug into a three or two prong outlet? This can indicate the age of the wiring.

Did you believe that this location was "haunted" when you moved in?

Were you told the location was possibly "haunted" when you moved in? Who told you?

What religious clergy may have been consulted?

Please give us a description of each of the events that you or anyone else in the home has experienced in your home

Who has witnessed these events (and what events have they witnessed?) that do not live in the home?

Have there been any unexplained odors?

What has been smelled, when was it and in what location of the home was it in and was it foul or good?

What unexplained sounds have heard by you or anyone else in the home?

What sound(s) have been heard by whom...when they were heard and in what location of the home they have been heard?

Has anyone heard any voices?

Please state what type of voice and what has been heard by whom...when they were heard and in what location of the home they have been heard:

Has there been any movement of objects?

Explain what has been moved, and if anyone actually watched it move or if it was just noticed it in a different spot

Have there been any unexplained hot or cold spots? If yes, please explain:

Have there been any personal attacks? If yes, please explain:

When and what was the very first occurrence of any phenomena?

What was the initial reaction to the phenomena?

What was the duration of any and all phenomena?

Who was first to witness the phenomena?

Were there any other witnesses?

What time of day was the first occurrence of the phenomena?

How often do any of the phenomena occur?

What are the patterns to any phenomena that are experienced such as a certain time of day or week?

Does anybody feel the occurrences have increased since they were first noticed? If so, in what way?

What is the strangest incident experienced so far?

What were the weather conditions when the phenomenon occurred?

What is the most frightening incident that you have experienced so far?

What do you and the occupants believe is happening?

Do all occupants agree that what is happening is paranormal or

Do the occupants believe in the supernatural?

If not…what do others believe is happening?

Do you have any desire to keep the phenomena from leaving? If you do, for what reason?

Are there pets in the home or business?

If so, please state the type of animal and how many of each type you have:

If you have a pet, has any pet or animal shown unexplained behavior? What?

How long have you had your pet or animal?

Have you done any type of "investigating" on your own? Please explain what you have done to investigate

What equipment you have used, what evidence have you found and what your results or findings have been?

What would you like to see come from our investigation?

Have you visited any haunted locations before; alone or in a group?

It is my hope that you enjoyed this book and were able to glean something of value, even if it's one idea that you can take with you on your next interview. There are many ideas on what's best when it comes to interviewing individuals. I tried to pass on information I have used throughout the years I learned as an investigator. No matter where it came from the information has helped me grow as an investigator. I continue to use this information on a daily basis.

CPSIA information can be obtained at www.ICGtesting.com
Printed in the USA
LVOW06s0411020514

384175LV00001B/165/P

9 781611 025903